THE PARISH CH...
T MARY THE V...

The Rector's Welcome

Visitors to a church like St Mary's can come as tourists, or as seekers, or as pilgrims. But the truth is that, in our own individual ways, we are probably all three.

As tourists we see this large, ancient church to be an impressive and fascinating historic building full of the varied past of Rye. As seekers we try to understand the motives and the ideals of those who have made their own personal contributions to this Christian place of worship over many years. As pilgrims we seek to grow spiritually in a world where material values often seem so important but give no ultimate satisfaction.

This guide has to be mainly concerned with the first two groups but, as pilgrims, do use the candle prayer stand and the fish prayer net.

In all three ways may your visit to St Mary's be enjoyable and memorable for you.

Martin Sheppard TEAM RECTOR

The Early Years

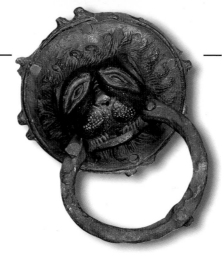

For almost 900 years the Parish Church of Rye, dedicated to St Mary the Virgin, has dominated the hill on which the old town stands.

The Domesday Book, completed in 1086, records 'The Abbot of Fécamp holds Rameslie from the King, and held it from King Edward … There are five churches and a new Borough with 64 Burgesses. Hastings has four.' It is almost certain that one of these churches was on or near the site of the present building, and that Rye was the new borough.

When the building of the present church was started, early in the 12th century, the town itself and much of the

Above right: The Sanctuary knocker, a copy of which is in the church.

Below: Norman arches on the west side of the north transept.

surrounding area was still held, under a Royal deed of gift, by the Abbey of Fécamp in Normandy. Fécamp was the first Norman monastery to own land in England. An early charter says that Ethelred II ('The Unready') planned to give 'Rameslie' to the monastery as a reward for giving him sanctuary from the Danes in 1014, but his death in 1016 prevented it. Canute, on gaining the kingdom, carried out the intentions of his old enemy, probably at the instigation of his new wife Queen Emma (the daughter of Duke Robert I of Normandy, and Ethelred's widow) in about 1017, the date of their marriage.

Fécamp Abbey was the favourite monastery of the Norman ducal house, and holding Rameslie, which included Rye, Winchelsea and Hastings as part of its extensive lands on the Sussex Coast, meant that it controlled one of the principal gateways to the Continent. William the Conqueror, Duke of Normandy, entered England through this 'Norman' land – with Fécamp monks in his party – to win the Battle of Hastings in 1066.

From acting as guides at the invasion across 'their' lands, the monks took

Right inset: One of the Norman animal heads in the north transept.

⑫

Right: The nave was built in the second half of the 12th century. The pillars and arches, though repaired, are original. The clerestory above the arches was rebuilt in 1882. The chancel, as well as the transepts, suffered severely in the raid of 1377, and the new piers and pointed arches were subsequently built in the style then prevailing.

Above: The two heads on the exterior of the north wall of the nave date from the 19th century.

a leading role in England for the next 150 years. One of their main influences was in reorganizing the Anglo-Norman Church and in rebuilding churches and cathedrals in the Norman manner – Rye for example! The original charter was granted by King Canute (1016–35) and was renewed from time to time by subsequent English monarchs until Henry III resumed possession in 1247. In exchange, he gave the Abbey certain lands which lay back from the coast and which could not be used as a base for the sort of invasion which had been staged by Louis, Dauphin of France, when he landed at Rye, without much resistance, in 1215.

It was the Abbot of Fécamp, William de Ros, who ordered the lavish rebuilding of the church, following a visit he paid to his English possessions in 1103. The chancel was built first and was probably completed in about 1120. Not much of the original structure now remains but its extent is marked by the two Norman aumbries (small recesses where the vessels used to celebrate Mass were kept) in the east wall and the transepts. He was at the same time engaged in building his own Abbey church in Fécamp, but died before the chancel of either project was completed.

The work on both churches was continued by Abbot Henry de Sully, a nephew of King Stephen of England. The two buildings were constructed on a similar cruciform plan with a long, rectangular chancel and a central tower.

Above: The Benedicite Window and the pendulum. The pendulum is 18 feet in length. Inset: There has always been a long pendulum in the church, though it has varied in length over the years. The present 'bob' was made by local clockmakers and is marked R Gill 1810.

Above: A view of Rye by Sir Anthony Van Dyck, dated 1633.

It is because of this link with Fécamp and the fact that it had become an important member of the Cinque Ports Confederation (towns which were allowed a certain amount of self-government – unusual in those feudal times – in return for supplying the king with a navy) that Rye has such a magnificent church, which has sometimes been called 'the Cathedral of East Sussex'.

Building in those days was a slow but thorough business. Construction of the nave, which completed the cruciform design, is thought to have commenced in about 1180. It was built during the so-called Transitional period, because the arcade arches become more and more pointed from east to west, until the last two, which are typically Early English and have traces of foliage on the capitals. It was over a hundred years after the construction of the chancel that the church was finally completed by the addition of the two side chapels. Although the basic design has survived, there have been many changes, both inside and out.

Right: Cannonballs found in the churchyard are evidence of Rye's turbulent history.

The worst disaster in its history occurred in 1377 when the town was looted and set on fire by French invaders and the church was extensively damaged. The roof fell in and the church bells were carried off to France. It appears that the people of Rye put up a rather feeble resistance and some of the leading inhabitants who had survived the incident were subsequently hanged and quartered as traitors by order of the Mayor and the King's Bailiff.

The next year the men of Rye and Winchelsea sailed to Normandy, set fire to two towns and recovered much of the loot, including the church bells – one of which was subsequently hung in Watchbell Street, to give warning of any future attack. It was not returned to the church until early in the 16th century.

Above: *The clock mechanism is one of the oldest church turret clocks still functioning and chimes the quarters and a single hourly toll.*

Right: *Cast in 1775, each bell bears the name of the makers, Pack and Chapman, and a rhyme. The bells were re-hung in 1995, and the church has an active bell-ringing team.*

The Tower

The bells are not the original ones stolen by the French in 1377 and subsequently recovered. In 1775 six of the then existing bells were re-cast and two new ones added. The total weight of the eight bells and clappers is nearly five tons.

The 'new' clock, made by the Huguenot Lewys Billiard in about 1561–2, is one of the oldest church turret clocks in the country still functioning. The pendulum, a much later addition, swings in the body of the church. The present exterior clock face and the original 'Quarter Boys' (so called because they strike the quarters but not the hours) were added in 1760.

Right: The golden weather vane at the top of the tower dates from 1703. The church tower has been used as a lookout from the day it was built and has been of assistance to sailors as a landmark to be seen from Dungeness to Fairlight.

Below: The red roofs of Rye from the tower, looking north.

Change and Decay

During the Reformation in the 16th century the interior of the church was stripped of its rood, images and ornaments, and much of the church property in the way of land was confiscated. In the reign of Queen Mary (1553–58), the roodloft and ornaments were restored but, on the accession of Queen Elizabeth I in 1558, the churchwardens dutifully removed them again.

From 1562 Rye willingly gave shelter to large numbers of Huguenots fleeing

Below: The North Chapel, built in the 13th century. Originally dedicated to St Nicholas, it is now known as the Clare Chapel. Here lies Allen Grebell (see over page). ⑭

from persecution in France, and in 1582 there were over 1,500 people of French extraction living in the town, whose total population was about 3,500. For a time they had their own ministers and held their own services in the church but, by the end of the century, they attended the ordinary services. In 1685 a further 50 Huguenot families arrived after the Revocation of the Edict of Nantes. Some of the Huguenots' descendants worship here to this day.

On the whole the inhabitants of Rye appear to have accepted civil and religious changes with

Left: One o the two orig inal 'Quarte Boys' or 'jack which stood above the clock dial. They have been replaced by fibre glass replicas.

Below: The Communion table in the Clar Chapel is an outstand ing example of carved mahogany, dating from about 1735. Presented by a memb of the Lamb family, i precise origin is unknown. The Lamb family was very influ ential in Rye for a period of 120 years, from 1715–1835.

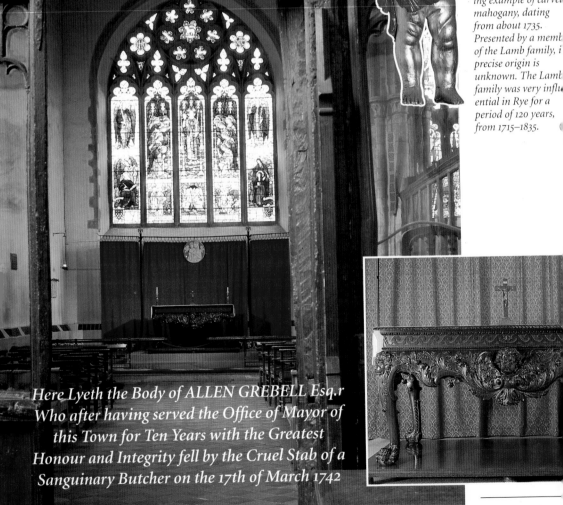

Here Lyeth the Body of ALLEN GREBELL Esq.r
Who after having served the Office of Mayor of
this Town for Ten Years with the Greatest
Honour and Integrity fell by the Cruel Stab of a
Sanguinary Butcher on the 17th of March 1742

nimity and to have attended what-
form of service they found proceed-
n their parish church. However, the
series of religious quarrels and the
of church revenues did lead to the
ect and decay of the building and in
ate 17th century the chancel was said
' 'very ruinous'.

1701 the vicar and churchwardens
ioned the king for financial assis-
e, saying the church was so ruinous
people were afraid to attend
ces. In the end, enough money was
d to complete the most essential
by the end of 1703.

ome thirty years later major repairs
again undertaken and in the ensu-
ears the churchwardens were
tantly patching the roof and dealing
minor repairs.

*ght: The flying buttresses. The nearest one
ates from the 15th century and was built to
upport the thrust of the new arcade. The
further one was erected in the last century.*

Below right: *The finely emblazoned Royal
Arms, hanging above the chancel arch, is
dated 1704 and bears the initials and
motto of Queen Anne.*   ⑦

Below: *The St George memorial to Vice
Admiral Sir George Warrender, who
died in 1917.*   ⑯

Smuggling and a Murder

By the middle of the 16th century, when more services took place in the nave rather than in the chancel, the north and south chancels were cut off from the main building. In 1569 guns and stores for the town were being kept in the south chancel and almost a century later, in 1637, a complaint was made that it contained 'arsenals, prisons and places of execution of punishment'.

Later the south chancel was divided into two floors, and the upper floor became a school for poor pupils. The remains of the school's fireplace can still be seen high up on the chancel wall.

The north chancel has been used for various purposes; as a lumber room, the home of the town's fire engine (which can now be seen in Rye Museum) and, it is rumoured, for hiding smuggled goods. However, until 1854 it continued to be used to bury people, and two of the graves feature in a famous Rye story. Next to each other lie Allen Grebell – murdered by mistake in 1742 by John Breeds – and members of the Lamb family, James Lamb having been the intended victim. The murder took place in the churchyard when John Breeds killed the deputy mayor instead of the mayor. Various explanations have been offered, including vengeance, mental illness, or the Rye smuggling mafia diverting attention from their activities. Nevertheless from 1792 to 1862 the murderer and his victim lay together in the north chancel, the remains of John Breeds' skeleton, in an iron cage, having been moved there from Gibbets Marsh. In 1862, when the chancel chapels were re-opened, the iron cage and its contents were removed to the attic of the Town Hall in Rye.

In 1882 an extensive restoration scheme was put in hand. There is no doubt that the building was once again in a very dilapidated state. The nave had been covered with a flat plaster ceiling, concealing the

Below: The water tower in the churchyard was built by the town and completed in 1735.

Below: The organ was built by Norman & Be and the case was made by local craftsmen. Installed in 1901, it cost £871.

fact that many of the clerestory windo were boarded up, and the walls were considered dangerous. With Victorian thoroughness the restorers set to, in o to put things right. The nave was re-roofed, an entirely new clerestory

There are three fine oil paintings in the church. In the north aisle, Mercy at the Wicket Gate *by C.P. Jacombe Hood MVO; in the south aisle,* The Adoration of the Magi *by Oswald Moser, RI; and, i the crossing,* Maternita *by Cinello.*

structed, the walls were strengthened,
west door blocked up and a clean
ep was made of much of the interior.
ome of this drastic reconstruction
been much criticised. Indeed, one
-known architect, who read a paper
Rye Parish Church to the Sussex
aeological Society in 1892, was
icularly incensed by what he consid-
to be the iconoclastic methods of
and 19th-century restorers. He said,
fect, that the church, as a historic
ding, had suffered more from their
guided zeal during the past 200 years
it had from the French and the
tans during previous centuries. It

*t: The Burne-Jones window in the north aisle
outstanding beauty. All the early stained glass
mashed during the Reformation.*

*w: The Mayor of Rye's chair. Until 1602 the
or was chosen in the churchyard on the
ay after St Bartholomew's Day and a plaque
e churchyard marks the probable site.*

is perhaps fortunate that plans to bring the transepts up to
Victorian standards were dropped.

The next major restoration programme was started after the
Second World War. Although the only visible damage sustained
by the church during the war was the loss of the East Window
from bomb blast, an inspection carried out after the cessation
of hostilities revealed that much of the fabric was in a very bad
state. In 1948 an extensive restoration programme was put in
hand and this is still going on.

Some of the repairs such as the rebuilding of the buttresses
on the south side are obvious. Others, like the major operation
of tying the north transept walls to the tower with reinforced

Left: A selection of
kneelers stitched by
ladies of the parish
over a period of
10 years.

Above: Captain Horatio Pugwash, the well-
known cartoon character by John Ryan who l...
in Rye. Shown above is 'Home and Rye!'.

Left: The West Window was presented in 1937
Mr E.F. Benson, the novelist and Mayor of Ry...
1934–36, in memory of his parents, Archbisho...
and Mrs Benson. The donor is in the bottom ...
corner, in his mayoral robes. His dog, Taffy,
appears in the centre, near the bottom.

concrete ringbeam and similar work ...
the wall of the upper room, are not vi...
ble. In addition, the entire roof has be...
restored, many of the timbers replace...
the tower strengthened and the floori...
of the nave renewed. Recent works ha...
included restoration to stonework an...
windows, and the re-opening of the
doors to 'The Upper Room' and to th...
tower from inside the church.

During the course of its long life t...
church has suffered from enemy actic...
from exposure to wind and rain, at ti...
from sheer neglect and, sadly, from il...
conceived and badly executed attemp...
at restoration. There are always repai...
be done, but it is hoped that never ag...
as in 1701, will the church be 'so ruind...
that the people are afraid to attend
services'.